STARTERS
MATHS

Going Places
Maths

Macdonald Educational

All these people are going somewhere.
How many are going a long way?
How many are in the set going by air?
2

People travel in different ways.
The astronaut travels in a spaceship.
Can you match a person
to each kind of transport?

3

What can you say about this set?
How many members are in the picture?
Does an aeroplane belong to this set?

4

Can you sort these into two sets?

How many travel on water?

How many fly in the air?

How many more has the sailing set?

There are buildings everywhere.
Look at the tall and the low buildings.
Can you see the shapes they make?
6

These buildings are in different countries.
Some buildings are symmetrical.
One side balances the other.
Are all these buildings symmetrical?

7

This village has a church.
The bus stop is one kilometre away.
What place is one kilometre
from your home?

8

BUS STOP

Here is a map of the village.
Find the church and the bus stop.
How long does it take you to walk
one kilometre from your house?

9

Here are some wheels
from long ago.
You can see how wheels
have changed.

10

Wheels help things to move easily.
When wheels turn we say they rotate.
One whole turn of a wheel
is called a revolution.

11

next coach for
LEEDS
leaves at 09.00

This coach holds 29 passengers.
How many seats will be empty?
When does the coach leave?

12

Arrivals		Departures	
Paris	09.00	Milan	09.30
Brussels	09.20	Paris	09.45
Rome	09.40	Bonn	10.00

08 | 45

luggage
allowance
20kg per person

These people are arriving at the airport.
A machine weighs their luggage.
What takes the luggage to the plane?

13

100 of these
are worth
1 of this

Each country has its own money.
Most countries use decimal currency.
One hundred pennies are worth
one pound.

The family are on holiday.
Father photographs the dog.
The picture can be made bigger.
The shape of the dog stays the same.

15

Mosaics are found in many countries.
Can you see the patterns they make?

16

Mosaics are made from tiny pieces
of stone.
Sometimes glass or marble is used.
Can you make mosaic pictures?

17

How many people will each car hold?
Which of these holds most people?
Arrange them in order of how many
they hold.

18

These crafts go at different speeds.
Which one goes very fast?
Which is slowest of all?

It is busy on the motorway.
Look at the junction.
Find the way along the roads
with your finger.

There are many signs on the roads.
They have shapes on them.
What do the shapes tell us?
What do these road signs mean?

In some countries it is very hot.
In others it is very cold.
How do we measure the temperature?

The time is different
at different places around the world.
We can measure time on a clock.
Can you make a clock to measure time?

23

Look at these vehicles.
Some are longer than others.
Which is longest of all?
Which two are the same length?

The white strip is 1 unit long.

How long are the others?

Which is the longest?

How many are shorter than the red one?

Can you count these groups of people?
What numeral goes in these boxes?

5,2 ⟶ ☐   3,6 ⟶ ☐   1,4 ⟶ ☐

26

Falling water makes lovely shapes
and patterns.
It is very strong, and has great force.

Index